By W. H. Auden

ABOUT THE HOUSE

RANDOM HOUSE
NEW YORK

ABOUT
THE HOUSE

W. H. AUDEN

Fourth Printing
© *Copyright, 1965, 1964, 1963, 1962, 1959, by W. H. Auden*
All rights reserved under International and Pan-American Copyright
Conventions. Published in New York by Random House, Inc., and
simultaneously in Toronto, Canada, by Random House of Canada Limited.
Library of Congress catalog card number: 65–15438

The following poems have appeared previously:

"Encomium Balnei," "The Cave of Nakedness," "A Change of Air,"
"Iceland Revisited," and "Transliterations #2, 3, and 4" (which appear
in this volume as "Volcanoes," "The Complaint Book," and "Parabolic
Ballad," under "Four Transliterations"), in Encounter;

"The Cave of Making," in The Listener;

"Hammerfest," and "Ascension Day, 1964," in The London Magazine;

"The Common Life," in The New York Review of Books;

"Thanksgiving for a Habitat," "On the Circuit," and "After Reading a
Child's Guide to Modern Physics," in The New Yorker;

"Whitsunday in Kirchstetten," in The Reporter;

"The Maker," in Poetry in Glass (Steuben Glass).

Manufactured in the United States of America
by The Haddon Craftsmen, Scranton, Pennsylvania
Designed by Betty Anderson

FOR

Edmund AND Elena

Wilson

A moon profaned by
Sectarian din, death by
Fervent implosion:—
Possibles. But here and now
Our oath to the living word.

Contents

Thanksgiving for a Habitat

In and Out

THANKSGIVING FOR A HABITAT

Funes ceciderunt mihi in praeclaris:
etenim hereditas mea praeclara est mihi.
Psalm XVI, 6

I

PROLOGUE: THE BIRTH OF ARCHITECTURE

(for John Bayley)

From gallery-grave and the hunt of a wren-king
    to Low Mass and trailer camp
is hardly a tick by the carbon clock, but I
    don't count that way nor do you:
already it is millions of heartbeats ago
    back to the Bicycle Age,
before which is no *After* for me to measure,
    just a still prehistoric *Once*
where anything could happen. To you, to me,
    Stonehenge and Chartres Cathedral,
the Acropolis, Blenheim, the Albert Memorial
    are works by the same Old Man
under different names: we know what He did,
    what, even, He thought He thought,
but we don't see why. (To get that, one would have
    to be selfish in His way,
without concrete or grapefruit.) It's our turn now
    to puzzle the unborn. No world
wears as well as it should but, mortal or not,
    a world has still to be built
because of what we can see from our windows,
    that Immortal Commonwealth
which is there regardless: It's in perfect taste
    and it's never boring but
it won't quite do. Among its populations
    are masons and carpenters
who build the most exquisite shelters and safes,
    but no architects, any more
than there are heretics or bounders: to take

[3]

umbrage at death, to construct
a second nature of tomb and temple, lives
must know the meaning of *If*.

Postscript

Some thirty inches from my nose
The frontier of my Person goes,
And all the untilled air between
Is private *pagus* or demesne.
Stranger, unless with bedroom eyes
I beckon you to fraternize,
Beware of rudely crossing it:
I have no gun, but I can spit.

II

THANKSGIVING FOR A HABITAT

(for Geoffrey Gorer)

Nobody I know would like to be buried
    with a silver cocktail shaker,
a transistor radio and a strangled
    daily help, or keep his word because

of a great-great-grandmother who got laid
    by a sacred beast. Only a press lord
could have built San Simeon: no unearned income
    can buy us back the gait and gestures

to manage a baroque staircase, or the art
    of believing footmen don't hear
human speech. (In adulterine castles
    our half-strong might hang their jackets

while mending their lethal bicycle chains:
    luckily, there are not enough
crags to go round.) Still, Hetty Pegler's Tump
    is worth a visit, so is Schönbrunn,

to look at someone's idea of the body
    that should have been his, as the flesh
Mum formulated shouldn't: that whatever
    he does or feels in the mood for,

stocktaking, horseplay, worship, making love,
    he stays the same shape, disgraces
a Royal I. To be overadmired is not
    good enough: although a fine figure

[5]

is rare in either sex, others like it
   have existed before. One may
be a Proustian snob or a sound Jacksonian
   democrat, but which of us wants

to be touched inadvertently, even
   by his beloved? We know all about graphs
and Darwin, enormous rooms no longer
   superhumanize, but earnest

city planners are mistaken: a pen
   for a rational animal
is no fitting habitat for Adam's
   sovereign clone. I, a transplant

from overseas, at last am dominant
   over three acres and a blooming
conurbation of country lives, few of whom
   I shall ever meet, and with fewer

converse. Linnaeus recoiled from the Amphibia
   as a naked gruesome rabble,
Arachnids give me the shudders, but fools
   who deface their emblem of guilt

are germane to Hitler: the race of spiders
   shall be allowed their webs. I should like
to be to my water-brethren as a spell
   of fine weather: Many are stupid,

and some, maybe, are heartless, but who is not
   vulnerable, easy to scare,
and jealous of his privacy? (I am glad
   the blackbird, for instance, cannot

tell if I'm talking English, German or
    just typewriting: that what he utters
I may enjoy as an alien rigmarole.) I ought
    to outlast the limber dragonflies

as the muscle-bound firs are certainly
    going to outlast me: I shall not end
down any esophagus, though I may succumb
    to a filter-passing predator,

shall, anyhow, stop eating, surrender my smidge
    of nitrogen to the World Fund
with a drawn-out *Oh* (unless at the nod
    of some jittery commander

I be translated in a nano-second
    to a c.c. of poisonous nothing
in a giga-death). Should conventional
    blunderbuss war and its routiers

invest my bailiwick, I shall of course
    assume the submissive posture:
but men are not wolves and it probably
    won't help. Territory, status,

and love, sing all the birds, are what matter:
    what I dared not hope or fight for
is, in my fifties, mine, a toft-and-croft
    where I needn't, ever, be at home *to*

those I am not at home *with*, not a cradle,
    a magic Eden without clocks,
and not a windowless grave, but a place
    I may go both in and out of.

III

THE CAVE OF MAKING
(In Memoriam Louis MacNeice)

For this and for all enclosures like it the archetype
    is Weland's Stithy, an antre
more private than a bedroom even, for neither lovers nor
    maids are welcome, but without a
bedroom's secrets: from the Olivetti portable,
    the dictionaries (the very
best money can buy), the heaps of paper, it is evident
    what must go on. Devoid of
flowers and family photographs, all is subordinate
    here to a function, designed to
discourage daydreams—hence windows averted from plausible
    videnda but admitting a light one
could mend a watch by—and to sharpen hearing: reached by an
    outside staircase, domestic
noises and odors, the vast background of natural
    life are shut off. Here silence
is turned into objects.
               I wish, Louis, I could have shown it you
    while you were still in public,
and the house and garden: lover of women and Donegal,
    from your perspective you'd notice
sights I overlook, and in turn take a scholar's interest
    in facts I could tell you (for instance,
four miles to our east, at a wood palisade, Carolingian
    Bavaria stopped, beyond it
unknowable nomads). Friends we became by personal
    choice, but fate had already
made us neighbors. For Grammar we both inherited
    good mongrel barbarian English

which never completely succumbed to the Roman rhetoric
  or the Roman gravity, that nonsense
which stood none. Though neither of our dads, like Horace's
  wiped his nose on his forearm,
neither was porphyry-born, and our ancestors probably
  were among those plentiful subjects
it cost less money to murder. Born so, both of us
  became self-conscious at a moment
when locomotives were named after knights in Malory,
  Science to schoolboys was known as
Stinks, and the Manor still was politically numinous:
  both watched with mixed feelings
the sack of Silence, the churches empty, the cavalry
  go, the Cosmic Model
become German, and any faith if we had it, in immanent
  virtue died. More than ever
life-out-there is goodly, miraculous, lovable,
  but we shan't, not since Stalin and Hitler,
trust ourselves ever again: we know that, subjectively,
  all is possible.
              To you, though,
ever since, last Fall, you quietly slipped out of Granusion,
  our moist garden, into
the Country of Unconcern, no possibility
  matters. I wish you hadn't
caught that cold, but the dead we miss are easier
  to talk to: with those no longer
tensed by problems one cannot feel shy and, anyway,
  when playing cards or drinking
or pulling faces are out of the question, what else is there
  to do but talk to the voices
of conscience they have become? From now on, as a visitor
  who needn't be met at the station,
your influence is welcome at any hour in my ubity,
  especially here, where titles

from *Poems* to *The Burning Perch* offer proof positive
    of the maker you were, with whom I
once collaborated, once at a weird Symposium
    exchanged winks as a juggins
went on about Alienation.
                          Who would, for preference,
    be a bard in an oral culture,
obliged at drunken feasts to improvise a eulogy
    of some beefy illiterate burner,
giver of rings, or depend for bread on the moods of a
    Baroque Prince, expected,
like his dwarf, to amuse? After all, it's rather a privilege
    amid the affluent traffic
to serve this unpopular art which cannot be turned into
    background noise for study
or hung as a status trophy by rising executives,
    cannot be "done" like Venice
or abridged like Tolstoy, but stubbornly still insists upon
    being read or ignored: our handful
of clients at least can rune. (It's heartless to forget about
    the underdeveloped countries,
but a starving ear is as deaf as a suburban optimist's:
    to stomachs only the Hindu
integers truthfully speak.) Our forerunners might envy us
    our remnant still able to listen:
as Nietzsche said they would, the *plebs* have got steadily
    denser, the *optimates*,
quicker still on the uptake. (Today, even Talleyrand
    might seem a naïf: he had so
little to cope with.) I should like to become, if possible,
    a minor atlantic Goethe,
with his passion for weather and stones but without his silliness
    re the Cross: at times a bore, but,
while knowing Speech can at best, a shadow echoing
    the silent light, bear witness
to the Truth it is not, he wished it were, as the Francophile

gaggle of pure songsters
are too vain to. We're not musicians: to stink of Poetry
   is unbecoming, and never
to be dull shows a lack of taste. Even a limerick
   ought to be something a man of
honor, awaiting death from cancer or a firing squad,
   could read without contempt: (at
that frontier I wouldn't dare speak to anyone
   in either a prophet's bellow
or a diplomat's whisper).

                    Seeing you know our mystery
   from the inside and therefore
how much, in our lonely dens, we need the companionship
   of our good dead, to give us
comfort on dowly days when the self is a nonentity
   dumped on a mound of nothing,
to break the spell of our self-enchantment when lip-smacking
   imps of mawk and hooey
write with us what they will, you won't think me imposing if
   I ask you to stay at my elbow
until cocktail time: dear Shade, for your elegy
   I should have been able to manage
something more like you than this egocentric monologue,
   but accept it for friendship's sake.

Postscript

   Timeless fictional worlds
   Of self-evident meaning
   Would not delight,

   Were not our own
   A temporal one where nothing
   Is what it seems.

               ◇ ◇ ◇

A poem—a tall story:
But any good one
Makes us want to know.

❖ ❖ ❖

Only tuneless birds,
Inarticulate warriors,
Need bright plumage.

❖ ❖ ❖

In a brothel, both
The ladies and gentlemen
Have nicknames only.

❖ ❖ ❖

Speechless Evil
Borrowed the language of Good
And reduced it to noise.

❖ ❖ ❖

A dry sad day.
What pirate falsehood
Has beheaded your stream of Truth?

❖ ❖ ❖

At lucky moments we seem on the brink
Of really saying what we think we think:
But, even then, an honest eye should wink.

❖ ❖ ❖

Nature, consistent and august,
Can't teach us what to write or do:
With Her the real is always true,
And what is true is also just.

❖ ❖ ❖

Time has taught you
                    how much inspiration
your vices brought you,
                        what imagination

can owe temptation
                    yielded to,
that many a fine
                    expressive line
would not have existed,
                         had you resisted:
as a poet, you
                    know this is true,
and though in Kirk
                         you sometimes pray
to feel contrite,
                    it doesn't work.
Felix Culpa, you say:
                         perhaps you're right.

You hope, yes,
                    your books will excuse you,
save you from hell:
                         nevertheless,
without looking sad,
                         without in any way
seeming to blame
                    (He doesn't need to,
knowing well
                    what a lover of art
like yourself pays heed to),
                              God may reduce you
on Judgment Day
                    to tears of shame,
reciting by heart
                    the poems you would
have written, had
                    your life been good.

IV

DOWN THERE

(for Irving Weiss)

A cellar underneath the house, though not lived in,
Reminds our warm and windowed quarters upstairs that
Caves water-scooped from limestone were our first dwellings,
A providential shelter when the Great Cold came,
Which woke our feel for somewhere fixed to come back to,
A hole by occupation made to smell human.

Self-walled, we sleep aloft, but still, at safe anchor,
Ride there on caves; lamplit we dine at street level:
But, deep in Mother Earth, beneath her key-cold cloak,
Where light and heat can never spcil what sun ripened,
In barrels, bottles, jars, we mew her kind commons,
Wine, beer, conserves and pickles, good at all seasons.

Encrust with years of clammy grime, the lair, maybe,
Of creepy-crawlies or a ghost, its flagstoned vault
Is not for girls: sometimes, to test their male courage,
A father sends the younger boys to fetch something
For Mother from down there; ashamed to whimper, hearts
    pounding,
They dare the dank steps, re-emerge with proud faces.

The rooms we talk and work in always look injured
When trunks are being packed, and when, without warning,
We drive up in the dark, unlock and switch lights on,
They seem put out: a cellar never takes umbrage;
It takes us as we are, explorers, homebodies,
Who seldom visit others when we don't need them.

V

UP THERE

(for Anne Weiss)

Men would never have come to need an attic.
Keen collectors of glass or Roman coins build
Special cabinets for them, dote on, index
Each new specimen: only women cling to
Items out of their past they have no use for,
Can't name now what they couldn't bear to part with.

Up there, under the eaves, in bulging boxes,
Hats, veils, ribbons, galoshes, programs, letters
Wait unworshiped (a starving spider spins for
The occasional fly): no clock recalls it
Once an hour to the household it's a part of,
No Saint's Day is devoted to its function.

All it knows of a changing world it has to
Guess from children, who conjure in its plenum,
Now an eyrie for two excited sisters,
Where, when Mother is bad, her rage can't reach them,
Now a schooner on which a lonely only
Boy sails north or approaches coral islands.

VI

THE GEOGRAPHY OF THE HOUSE

(for Christopher Isherwood)

Seated after breakfast
In this white-tiled cabin
Arabs call *the House where
Everybody goes*,
Even melancholics
Raise a cheer to Mrs.
Nature for the primal
Pleasures She bestows.

Sex is but a dream to
Seventy-and-over,
But a joy proposed un-
   -til we start to shave:
Mouth-delight depends on
Virtue in the cook, but
This She guarantees from
Cradle unto grave.

Lifted off the potty,
Infants from their mothers
Hear their first impartial
Words of worldly praise:
Hence, to start the morning
With a satisfactory
Dump is a good omen
All our adult days.

Revelation came to
Luther in a privy
(Crosswords have been solved there)
Rodin was no fool
When he cast his Thinker,
Cogitating deeply,
Crouched in the position
Of a man at stool.

All the Arts derive from
This ur-act of making,
Private to the artist:
Makers' lives are spent
Striving in their chosen
Medium to produce a
De-narcissus-ized en-
    -during excrement.

Freud did not invent the
Constipated miser:
Banks have letter boxes
Built in their façade,
Marked *For Night Deposits*,
Stocks are firm or liquid,
Currencies of nations
Either soft or hard.

Global Mother, keep our
Bowels of compassion
Open through our lifetime,
Purge our minds as well:
Grant us a kind ending, .
Not a second childhood,
Petulant, weak-sphinctered,
In a cheap hotel.

Keep us in our station:
When we get pound-noteish,
When we seem about to
Take up Higher Thought,
Send us some deflating
Image like the pained ex-
    -pression on a Major
Prophet taken short.

(Orthodoxy ought to
Bless our modern plumbing:
Swift and St. Augustine
Lived in centuries,
When a stench of sewage
Ever in the nostrils
Made a strong debating
Point for Manichees.)

Mind and Body run on
Different timetables:
Not until our morning
Visit here can we
Leave the dead concerns of
Yesterday behind us,
Face with all our courage
What is now to be.

VII

ENCOMIUM BALNEI
(for Neil Little)

it is odd that the English
                              a rather dirty people
         should have invented the slogan
Cleanliness is next to Godliness
                                 meaning by that
         a gentleman smells faintly of tar
persuaded themselves that constant cold hydropathy
         would make the sons of gentlemen
pure in heart
                  (not that papa or his chilblained offspring can
         hope to be gentry)
                           still John Bull's
hip-bath it was
                     that made one carnal pleasure lawful
         for the first time since we quarreled
over Faith and Works
                        (Shakespeare probably stank
                                        Le Grand
         Monarque certainly did)
                              thanks to him
shrines where a subarctic fire-cult could meet and marry
         a river-cult from torrid Greece
rose again
                 resweetened the hirsute West
                                        a Roman though
         bath addict
                     amphitheater fan
would be puzzled
                     seeing the caracallan acreage

                    compressed into such a few square feet
mistake them for hideouts
                              warrens of some outlawed sect
          who mortify their flesh with strange
implements
               he is not that wrong
                              if the tepidarium's
          barrel vaulting has migrated
to churches and railroad stations
                                   if we no longer
          go there to wrestle or gossip
or make love
                    (you cannot purchase a conjugal tub)
          St. Anthony and his wild brethren
(for them ablutions were tabu
                              a habit of that doomed
          behavioral sink this world)
                              have been
just as he thought
               at work
                         we are no more chaste
                                             obedient
     nor
          if we can possibly help it
poor than he was but
                         enthusiasts who were have taught us
     (besides showing lovers of nature
how to carry binoculars instead of a gun)
          the unclassical wonder of being
all by oneself
                    though our dwellings may still have a master
          who owns the front-door key
                         a bathroom
has only an inside lock
                    belongs today to whoever

is taking a bath
          among us
to withdraw from the tribe at will
               be neither Parent
    Spouse nor Guest
          is a sacrosanct
political right
        where else shall the Average Ego
   find its peace
        not in dreams surely
the several worlds we invent as quite as pugnacious
   as the one into which we are born
and even more public
         on Oxford Street or Broadway
   I may escape notice
        but never
on roads I dream of
        what Eden is there for the lapsed
  but hot water
       snug in its caul
widows
   orphans
      exiles may feel as self-important
  as an only child
      and a sage
be silly without shame
       present a Lieder Abend
  to a captive audience of his toes
retreat from rhyme and reason into some mallarmesque
  syllabic fog
     for half an hour
it is wise to forget the time
      our daily peril
  and each other
    good for the soul

[21]

once in the twenty-four hour cycle of her body
    whether according to our schedule
as we sit down to breakfast
                  or stand up to welcome
   folk for dinner
          to feel as if
the Pilgrim's Way
         or as some choose to call it
                the War Path
   were now a square in the Holy City
that what was wrong has been put right
             as if Von Hügel's
  hoggers and lumpers were extinct
thinking the same as thanking
          all military hardware
   already slighted and submerged

VIII

GRUB FIRST, THEN ETHICS (Brecht)

(for Margaret Gardiner)

Should the shade of Plato
 visit us, anxious to know
how *anthropos* is, we could say to him: "Well,
 we can read to ourselves, our use
of holy numbers would shock you, and a poet
 may lament—where is Telford
whose bridged canals are still a Shropshire glory,
 where Muir who on a Douglas spruce
rode out a storm and called an earthquake noble,
 where Mr. Vynyian Board,
thanks to whose lifelong fuss the hunted whale now suffers
 a quicker death?—without being
called an idiot, though none of them bore arms or
 made a public splash," then "Look!"
we would point, for a dig at Athens, "Here
 is the place where we cook."

Though built in Lower Austria,
 do-it-yourself America
prophetically blueprinted this
 palace kitchen for kingdoms
where royalty would be incognito, for an age when
 Courtesy might think: "From your voice
and the back of your neck I know we shall get on
 but cannot tell from your thumbs

(N.B. Under the title "On Installing an American Kitchen in Lower
Austria," this poem appeared in my previous volume *Homage to Clio*. At
that time, I did not realize that its proper place was in a cycle.)

[23]

who is to give the orders." The right note is harder
        to hear than in the Age of Poise
when She talked shamelessly to her maid and sang
        noble lies with Him, but struck
it can be still in New Cnossos where if I am
        banned by a shrug it is my fault,
    not Father's, as it is my taste whom
        I put below the salt.

        The prehistoric hearthstone,
        round as a birthday-button
    and sacred to Granny, is as old
        stuff as the bowel-loosening
nasal war cry, but this all-electric room
        where ghosts would feel uneasy,
a witch at a loss, is numinous and again
        the center of a dwelling
not, as lately it was, an abhorrent dungeon
        where the warm unlaundered meiny
belched their comic prose and from a dream of which
        chaste Milady awoke blushing.
House-proud, deploring labor, extolling work,
        these engines politely insist
    that banausics can be liberals,
        a cook a pure artist

        who moves everyman
        at a deeper level than
    Mozart, for the subject of the verb
        to-hunger is never a name:
dear Adam and Eve had different bottoms,
        but the neotene who marches
upright and can subtract reveals a belly
        like the serpent's with the same

vulnerable look. Jew, Gentile or pigmy,
  he must get his calories
before he can consider her profile or
  his own, attack you or play chess,
and take what there is however hard to get down:
  then surely those in whose creed
  God is edible may call a fine
   omelette a Christian deed.

  The sin of Gluttony
   is ranked among the Deadly
  Seven, but in murder mysteries
   one can be sure the gourmet
didn't do it: children, brave warriors out of a job,
  can weigh pounds more than they should
and one can dislike having to kiss them yet,
  compared with the thin-lipped, they
are seldom detestable. Some waiter grieves
  for the worst dead bore to be a good
trencherman, and no wonder chefs mature into
  choleric types, doomed to observe
Beauty peck at a master-dish, their one reward
  to behold the mutually hostile
  mouth and eyes of a sinner married
   at the first bite by a smile.

  The houses of our City
   are real enough but they lie
  haphazardly scattered over the earth,
   and her vagabond forum
is any space where two of us happen to meet
  who can spot a citizen
without papers. So, too, can her foes. Where the
  power lies remains to be seen,

the force, though, is clearly with them: perhaps only
    by falling can She become
Her own vision, but we have sworn under four eyes
    to keep Her up—all we ask for,
should the night come when comets blaze and meres break,
    is a good dinner, that we
  may march in high fettle, left foot first,
    to hold her Thermopylae.

IX

FOR FRIENDS ONLY

(for John and Teckla Clark)

Ours yet not ours, being set apart
As a shrine to friendship,
Empty and silent most of the year,
This room awaits from you
What you alone, as visitor, can bring,
A weekend of personal life.

In a house backed by orderly woods,
Facing a tractored sugar-beet country,
Your working hosts engaged to their stint,
You are unlike to encounter
Dragons or romance: were drama a craving,
You would not have come.

Books we do have for almost any
Literate mood, and notepaper, envelopes,
For a writing one (to "borrow" stamps
Is a mark of ill-breeding):
Between lunch and tea, perhaps a drive;
After dinner, music or gossip.

Should you have troubles (pets will die,
Lovers are always behaving badly)
And confession helps, we will hear it,
Examine and give our counsel:
If to mention them hurts too much,
We shall not be nosey.

Easy at first, the language of friendship
Is, as we soon discover,
Very difficult to speak well, a tongue
With no cognates, no resemblance
To the galimatias of nursery and bedroom,
Court rhyme or shepherd's prose,

And, unless often spoken, soon goes rusty.
Distance and duties divide us,
But absence will not seem an evil
If it make our re-meeting
A real occasion. Come when you can:
Your room will be ready.

In Tum-Tum's reign a tin of biscuits
On the bedside table provided
For nocturnal munching. Now weapons have changed,
And the fashion in appetites:
There, for sunbathers who count their calories,
A bottle of mineral water.

Felicissima notte! May you fall at once
Into a cordial dream, assured
That whoever slept in this bed before
Was also someone we like,
That within the circle of our affection
Also you have no double.

X

TONIGHT AT SEVEN-THIRTY
(for M. F. K. Fisher)

    The life of plants
  is one continuous solitary meal,
      and ruminants
hardly interrupt theirs to sleep or to mate, but most
      predators feel
ravenous most of the time and competitive
always, bolting such morsels as they can contrive
to snatch from the more terrified: pack-hunters do
    dine *en famille*, it is true,
with protocol and placement, but none of them play host
  to a stranger whom they help first. Only man,
    supererogatory beast,
  Dame Kind's thoroughbred lunatic, can
      do the honors of a feast,

      and was doing so
  before the last Glaciation when he offered
      mammoth-marrow
and, perhaps, Long Pig, will continue till Doomsday
      when at God's board
the saints chew pickled Leviathan. In this age farms
are no longer crenellated, only cops port arms,
but the Law of the Hearth is unchanged: a brawler may not
    be put to death on the spot,
but he is asked to quit the sacral dining area
  instanter, and a foul-mouth gets the cold
    shoulder. The right of a guest
  to standing and foster is as old
    as the ban on incest.

                For authentic
        comity the gathering should be small
            and unpublic:
at mass banquets where flosculent speeches are made
            in some hired hall
we think of ourselves or nothing. Christ's cenacle
seated a baker's dozen, King Arthur's rundle
the same, but today, when one's host may well be his own
        chef, servitor and scullion,
when the cost of space can double in a decade,
    even that holy Zodiac number is
        too large a frequency for us:
    in fact, six lenient semble sieges,
            none of them perilous,

        is now a Perfect
    Social Number. But a dinner party,
        however select,
is a worldly rite that nicknames or endearments
        or family
diminutives would profane: two doters who wish
to tiddle and curmurr between the soup and fish
belong in restaurants, all children should be fed
        earlier and be safely in bed.
Well-liking, though, is a must: married maltalents
    engaged in some covert contrast can spoil
        an evening like the glance
    of a single failure in the toil
        of his bosom grievance.

        Not that a god,
    immune to grief, would be an ideal guest:
        he would be too odd
to talk to and, despite his imposing presence, a bore,
        for the funniest

mortals and the kindest are those who are most aware
of the baffle of being, don't kid themselves our care
is consolable, but believe a laugh is less
        heartless than tears, that a hostess
prefers it. Brains evolved after bowels, therefore,
    great assets as fine raiment and good looks
        can be on festive occasions,
    they are not essential like artful cooks
        and stalwart digestions.

        I see a table
    at which the youngest and oldest present
        keep the eye grateful
for what Nature's bounty and grace of Spirit can create:
        for the ear's content
one raconteur, one gnostic with amazing shop,
both in a talkative mood but knowing when to stop,
and one wide-traveled worldling to interject now and then
        a sardonic comment, men
and women who enjoy the cloop of corks, appreciate
    depatical fare, yet can see in swallowing
        a sign act of reverence,
    in speech a work of re-presenting
        the true olamic silence.

XI

THE CAVE OF NAKEDNESS
(for Louis and Emmie Kronenberger)

Don Juan needs no bed, being far too impatient to undress,
nor do Tristan and Isolda, much too in love to care
    for so mundane a matter, but unmythical
mortals require one, and prefer to take their clothes off,
    if only to sleep. That is why bedroom farces
must be incredible to be funny, why Peeping Toms
    are never praised, like novelists or bird watchers,
for their keenness of observation: where there's a bed,
    be it a nun's restricted cot or an Emperor's
baldachined and nightly-redamselled couch, there are no
    effable data. (Dreams may be repeatable,
but our deeds of errantry in the wilderness of wish
    so often turn out, when told, to be less romantic
than our day's routine: besides, we cannot describe them
    without faking.) Lovers don't see their embraces
as a viable theme for debate, nor a monk his prayers
    (do they, in fact, remember them?): O's of passion,
interior acts of attention, not being a story
    in which the names don't matter but the way of telling,
with a lawyer's wit or a nobleman's assurance,
    does, need a drawing room of their own. Bed-sitting-rooms
soon drive us crazy, a dormitory even sooner
    turns us to brutes: bona fide architects know
that doors are not emphatic enough, and interpose,
    as a march between two realms, so alien, so disjunct,
the no-man's-land of a stair. The switch from personage,
    with a state number, a first and family name,
to the naked Adam or Eve, and vice versa,
    should not be off-hand or abrupt: a stair retards it
to a solemn procession.

Since my infantile entrance
at my mother's bidding into Edwardian England,
I have suffered the transit over forty thousand times,
usually, to my chagrin, by myself: about
blended flesh, those midnight colloquia of Derbies and Joans,
I know nothing therefore, about certain occult
antipathies perhaps too much. Some perks belong, though
to all unwilling celibates: our rooms are seldom
battlefields, we enjoy the pleasure of reading in bed
(as we grow older, it's true, we may find it prudent
to get nodding drunk first), we retain the right to choose
our sacred image. (That I often start with sundry
splendors at sundry times greened after, but always end
aware of one, the same one, may be of no importance,
but I hope it is.) Ordinary human unhappiness
is life in its natural color, to cavil
putting on airs: at day-wester to think of nothing
benign to memorize is as rare as feeling
no personal blemish, and Age, despite its damage,
is well-off. When they look in their bedroom mirrors,
Fifty-plus may be bored, but Seventeen is faced by
a frowning failure, with no money, no mistress,
no manner of his own, who never got to Italy
nor met a great one: to say a few words at banquets,
to attend a cocktail party in honor of N or M,
can be severe, but Junior has daily to cope
with ghastly family meals, with dear Papa and Mama
being odd in the wrong way. (It annoys him to speak,
and it hurts him not to.)
                    When I disband from the world,
and entrust my future to the Gospel Makers,
I need not fear (not in neutral Austria) being called for
in the waist of the night by deaf agents, never
to be heard of on earth again: the assaults I would be spared
are none of them princely—fire, nightmare, insomnia's

Vision of Hell, when Nature's wholesome genial fabric
    lies utterly discussed and from a sullen vague
wafts a contagious stench, her adamant minerals
    all corrupt, each life a worthless iteration
of the general loathing (to know that, probably,
    its cause is chemical can degrade the panic,
not stint it). As a rule, with pills to help them, the Holy Four
    exempt my nights from nuisance, and even wake me
when I would be woken, when, audible here and there
    in the half-dark, members of an avian orchestra
are already softly noodling, limbering up for
    an overture at sunrise, their effort to express
in the old convention they inherit that joy in beginning
    for which our species was created, and declare it
good.

        We may not be obliged—though it is mannerly—to bless
    the Trinity that we are corporal contraptions,
but only a villain will omit to thank Our Lady or
    her henwife, Dame Kind, as he, she, or both ensemble,
emerge from a private cavity to be reborn,
    reneighbored in the Country of Consideration.

Postscript

Only look in the glass to detect a removable blemish:
As for the permanent ones, already you know quite enough.

                ❖   ❖   ❖

            Our bodies cannot love:
            But, without one,
            What works of Love could we do?

                ❖   ❖   ❖

Money cannot buy
The fuel of Love:
But is excellent kindling.

⬦ ⬦ ⬦

Nightmare of the base,
Silence to lovers
Is the welcome third party.

⬦ ⬦ ⬦

No winter in Dreamland:
Thermometers there
Stand always at blood-heat.

⬦ ⬦ ⬦

Since he weighs nothing,
Even the stoutest dreamer
Can fly without wings.

⬦ ⬦ ⬦

To dreamers who never
Travel by rail, I must be
An old fogey.

XII

THE COMMON LIFE
(for Chester Kallman)

A living room, the catholic area you
    (Thou, rather) and I may enter
without knocking, leave without a bow, confronts
    each visitor with a style,

a secular faith: he compares its dogmas
    with his, and decides whether
he would like to see more of us. (Spotless rooms
    where nothing's left lying about

chill me, so do cups used for ashtrays or smeared
    with lipstick: the homes I warm to,
though seldom wealthy, always convey a feeling
    of bills being promptly settled

with checks that don't bounce.) There's no *We* at an instant,
    only *Thou* and *I*, two regions
of protestant being which nowhere overlap:
    a room is too small, therefore,

if its occupants cannot forget at will
    that they are not alone, too big
if it gives them any excuse in a quarrel
    for raising their voices. What,

quizzing ours, would Sherlock Holmes infer? Plainly,
    ours is a sitting culture
in a generation which prefers comfort
    (or is forced to prefer it)

to command, would rather incline its buttocks
    on a well-upholstered chair
than the burly back of a slave: a quick glance
    at book titles would tell him

that we belong to the clerisy and spend much
    on our food. But could he read
what our prayers and jokes are about, what creatures
    frighten us most, or what names

head our roll call of persons we would least like
    to go to bed with? What draws
singular lives together in the first place,
    loneliness, lust, ambition,

or mere convenience, is obvious, why they drop
    or murder one another
clear enough: how they create, though, a common world
    between them, like Bombelli's

impossible yet useful numbers, no one
    has yet explained. Still, they do
manage to forgive impossible behavior,
    to endure by some miracle

conversational tics and larval habits
    without wincing (were you to die,
I should miss yours). It's a wonder that neither
    has been butchered by accident,

or, as lots have, silently vanished into
    History's criminal noise
unmourned for, but that, after twenty-four years,
    we should sit here in Austria

as cater-cousins, under the glassy look
    of a Naples Bambino,
the portrayed regards of Strauss and Stravinsky,
    doing British crossword puzzles,

is very odd indeed. I'm glad the builder gave
    our common-room small windows
through which no observed outsider can observe us:
    every home should be a fortress,

equipped with all the very latest engines
    for keeping Nature at bay,
versed in all ancient magic, the arts of quelling
    the Dark Lord and his hungry

animivorous chimeras. (Any brute
    can buy a machine in a shop,
but the sacred spells are secret to the kind,
    and if power is what we wish

they won't work.) *The ogre will come in any case:*
    so Joyce has warned us. Howbeit,
fasting or feasting, we both know this: without
    the Spirit we die, but life

without the Letter is in the worst of taste,
    and always, though truth and love
can never really differ, when they seem to,
    the subaltern should be truth.

IN AND OUT

We've covered ground since that awkward day
When, thoughtlessly, a human mind
Decided to leave the apes behind,
Come pretty far, but who dare say
If far be forward or astray,
Or what we still might do in the way
Of patient building, impatient crime,
Given the sunlight, salt and time.

Corns, heartburn, sinus headaches, such minor ailments
Tell of estrangement between your name and you,
Advise a change of air: heed them, but let
The modesty of their discomfort warn you
Against the flashy errands of your dreams.

To grow a sailor's beard, don monkish garb,
Or trade in an agglutinative tongue
With a stone-age culture, would be mollycoddling:
To go Elsewhere is to withdraw from movement,
A side step, a short one, will convey you thither.

Although its chaffinches, maybe, have learned
The dialect of another river basin,
A fault transformed the local building stone,
It has a priest, a postmistress, an usher,
Its children know they are not to beg from strangers.

Within its average elsewhereishness
Your name is as a mirror answers, yourself
How you behave in shops, the tips you give:
It sides with neither, being outside both,
But welcomes both with healing disregard.

Nor, when you both return here (for you will)
Where luck and instinct originally brought you,
Will it salute your reconciliation
With farewell rites, or populate your absence
With reverent and irreverent anecdote.

No study of your public reappearance
Will show, as judgment on a cure demands,
A sudden change in love, ideas, or diet:
Your sojourn Elsewhere will remain a wordless
Hiatus in your voluble biography.

Fanatic scholarship at most may prove
That you resigned from some Committee, unearth
A letter from the Grand Duke to his cousin,
Remarking, among more important gossip,
That you seem less amusing than you were.

Really, must you,
Over-familiar
Dense companion,
Be there always?
The bond between us
Is chimerical surely:
Yet I cannot break it.

Must I, born for
Sacred play,
Turn base mechanic
So you may worship
Your secular bread,
With no thought
Of the value of time?

Thus far I have known your
Character only
From its pleasanter side,
But you know I know
A day will come
When you grow savage
And hurt me badly.

Totally stupid?
Would that you were:
But, no, you plague me
With tastes I was fool enough
Once to believe in.
Bah!, blockhead:
I know where you learned them.

Can I trust you even
On creaturely fact?
I suspect strongly
You hold some dogma
Of positive truth,
And feed me fictions:
I shall never prove it.

Oh, I know how you came by
A sinner's cranium,
How between two glaciers
The master-chronometer
Of an innocent primate
Altered its tempi:
That explains nothing.

Who tinkered and why?
Why am I certain,
Whatever your faults are,
The fault is mine,
Why is loneliness not
A chemical discomfort,
Nor Being a smell?

Who, now, seeing Her so
Happily married,
Housewife, helpmate to Man,

Can imagine the screeching
Virago, the Amazon,
Earth Mother was?

Her jungle growths
Are abated,
Her exorbitant monsters abashed,

Her soil mumbled,
Where crops, aligned precisely,
Will soon be orient:

Levant or couchant,
Well-daunted thoroughbreds
Graze on mead and pasture,

A church clock subdivides the day,
Up the lane at sundown
Geese podge home.

As for Him:
What has happened to the Brute
Epics and nightmares tell of?

No bishops pursue
Their archdeacons with axes,
In the crumbling lair

Of a robber baron
Sightseers picnic
Who carry no daggers.

I well might think myself
A humanist,
Could I manage not to see

How the autobahn
Thwarts the landscape
In godless Roman arrogance,

The farmer's children
Tiptoe past the shed
Where the gelding knife is kept.

For over forty years I'd paid it atlas homage,
　　The northernmost township on earth, producing
The best deep-frozen fish sticks you can buy: for three days,
　　I pottered round, a monolingual pilgrim,
And drank the beer of the world's most northern brewery.
　　Though miles beyond the Moral Circle, I saw
No orgies, no great worms, nor dreamed of any during
　　Three sunny nights: louts, though—German this time—
Had left their usual mark. How much reverence could I,
　　Can anyone past fifty, afford to lose?

Was it as worldly as it looked? I might have thought so
　　But for my ears: something odd was happening
Soundwise. A word, a laugh, a footstep, a truck's outcry,
　　Each utterance rang singular, staccato,
To be cut off before it could be contradicted
　　Or confused by others: a listening terrain
Seized on them all and never gave one back in echo,
　　As if to land as desolate, as far up,
Whatever noise our species cared to make still mattered.
　　Here was a place we had yet to disappoint.

The only communities it had to judge us by
　　Were cenobite, mosses and lichen, sworn to
Station and reticence: its rocks knew almost nothing,
　　Nothing about the glum Reptilian Empire
Or the epic journey of the Horse, had heard no tales
　　Of that preglacial Actium when the huge

(N.B. *The Moral Circle:* a jocular term, used by southern Norwegians,
for the Arctic Circle. *German this time:* in 1945 the retreating *Wehr-
macht* burnt down every single house.)

[47]

Archaic shrubs went down before the scented flowers,
    And earth was won for color. For all it knew,
Religion had begun with the Salvation Army,
    Warfare with motorized resentful conscripts.

Ground so bare might take a century to realize
    How we behave to regions or to beings
Who have anything we're after: to have disgusted
    Millions of acres of good-natured topsoil
Is an achievement of a sort, to fail to notice
    How garden plants and farmyard beasts look at us,
Or refuse to look, to picture all of them as dear
    Faithful old retainers, another, but why
Bring that up now? My intrusion had not profaned it:
    If innocence is holy, it was holy.

ICELAND REVISITED

(for Basil and Susan Boothby)

Unwashed, unshat,
He was whisked from the plane
To a lunch in his honor.

❖ ❖ ❖

He hears a loudspeaker
Call him well-known:
But knows himself no better.

❖ ❖ ❖

Twenty-eight years ago
Three slept well here.
Now one is married, one dead,

Where the harmonium stood
A radio:—
Have the Fittest survived?

❖ ❖ ❖

Unable to speak Icelandic,
He helped instead
To do the dishes.

❖ ❖ ❖

The bondi's sheep dog
And the visitor from New York
Conversed freely.

❖ ❖ ❖

Snow had camouflaged
The pool of liquid manure:
The town mouse fell in.

❖ ❖ ❖

The desolate fjord
Denied the possibility
Of many gods.

❖ ❖ ❖

A blizzard. A bare room.
Thoughts of the past.
He forgot to wind his watch.

❖ ❖ ❖

The gale howled over lava. Suddenly
In the storm's eye
A dark speck,

Perseus in an air-taxi,
Come to snatch
Shivering Andromeda

Out of the wilderness
And bring her back
To hot baths, cocktails, habits.

❖ ❖ ❖

Once more
A child's dream verified
The magical light beyond Hekla.

❖ ❖ ❖

Fortunate island,
Where all men are equal
But not vulgar—not yet.

ON THE CIRCUIT

Among pelagian travelers,
Lost on their lewd conceited way
To Massachusetts, Michigan,
Miami or L.A.,

An airborne instrument I sit,
Predestined nightly to fulfill
Columbia-Giesen-Management's
Unfathomable will,

By whose election justified,
I bring my gospel of the Muse
To fundamentalists, to nuns,
To Gentiles and to Jews,

And daily, seven days a week,
Before a local sense has jelled,
From talking-site to talking-site
Am jet-or-prop-propelled.

Though warm my welcome everywhere,
I shift so frequently, so fast,
I cannot now say where I was
The evening before last,

Unless some singular event
Should intervene to save the place,
A truly asinine remark,
A soul-bewitching face,

Or blessed encounter, full of joy,
Unscheduled on the Giesen Plan,
With, here, an addict of Tolkein,
There, a Charles Williams fan.

Since Merit but a dunghill is,
I mount the rostrum unafraid:
Indeed, 'twere damnable to ask
If I am overpaid.

Spirit is willing to repeat
Without a qualm the same old talk,
But Flesh is homesick for our snug
Apartment in New York.

A sulky fifty-six, he finds
A change of mealtime utter hell,
Grown far too crotchety to like
A luxury hotel.

The Bible is a goodly book
I always can peruse with zest,
But really cannot say the same
For Hilton's *Be My Guest*,

Nor bear with equanimity
The radio in students' cars,
Musak at breakfast, or—dear God!—
Girl-organists in bars.

Then, worst of all, the anxious thought,
Each time my plane begins to sink
And the No Smoking sign comes on:
What will there be to drink?

Is this a milieu where I must
How grahamgreeneish! How infra dig!
Snatch from the bottle in my bag
An analeptic swig?

Another morning comes: I see,
Dwindling below me on the plane,
The roofs of one more audience
I shall not see again.

God bless the lot of them, although
I don't remember which was which:
God bless the U.S.A., so large,
So friendly, and so rich.

I

A TOAST

(Christ Church Gaudy, 1960)

What on earth does one say at a Gaudy,
 On such an occasion as this,
O what, since I may not be bawdy,
 Can I do except reminisce?
Middle-age with its glasses and dentures
 (There's an opera about it by Strauss)
Puts an end to romantic adventures,
 But not to my love of *The House*.

Ah! those Twenties before I was twenty,
 When the news never gave one the glooms,
When the chef had minions in plenty,
 And we could have lunch in our rooms.
In *Peck* there were marvelous parties
 With bubbly and brandy and grouse,
And the aesthetes fought with the hearties:
 It was fun, then, to be at *The House*.

National Service had not been suggested,
 O-Level and A were called Certs,
Our waistcoats were cut double-breasted,
 Our flannel trousers like skirts.
One could meet any day in Society
 Harold Acton, Tom Driberg or *Rowse:*
May there always, to lend their variety,
 Be some rather odd fish at *The House*.

The *Clarendon*'s gone—I regret her—
  The *George* is closed and forgot;
Some changes are all for the better,
  But *Woolworth*'s is probably not.
May the *Meadows* be only frequented
  By scholars and couples and cows:
God save us from all these demented
  Plans for a road through *The House*.

All those who wish well to our College
  Will wish her *Treasurer* well;
May Mammon give him foreknowledge
  Of just what to buy and to sell,
That all his investments on which her
  Income depends may be wows:
May She ever grow richer and richer,
  And the gravy abound at *The House*.

God bless and keep out of quarrels
  The *Dean*, the *Chapter* and *D*,
The *Censors* who shepherd our morals,
  Roy, *Hooky*, *Little* and me.
May those who come up next October
  Be *anständig*, have *esprit* and *nous*:
And now, though not overly sober,
  I give you a toast—TO THE HOUSE!

II

A SHORT ODE TO A PHILOLOGIST
(*1962*)

Die Sprache ist die Mutter, nicht die Magd, des Gedankens.
—K. Kraus

Necessity knows no Speech. Not even
Shakespeare can say
What must be said so well as Frisch's bees convey
Vital instructions by ballet,
Nor do Jack and Jill, like thrushes,
Grow outspoken under May's compulsion:
A scream can be uncontrollable, and yawning a rudeness
One has to be excused, but free
Speech is a tautology.

Who means *Good Morning* reveals he is not
Napoleon or
Napoleon's cook, but quite as born, a new author,
Ready in turn to answer for
A story he cannot invent
But must leave to others to tell with what
Prejudice they prefer. Social climbers daren't invite comment,
And a chatterbox doesn't: in
Speech, if true, true deeds begin.

If not, there's International Babel,
In which murders
Are sanitary measures and stockbrokers
Integrity-ridden, for sirs
Who think big, where noises abound
For throats to hire whose doom is to compel
Attention: Its Void costs money, being flood-lit, wired for sound,
With banner headlines guaranteed,
And applause prerecorded.

[56]

But Dame Philology is our Queen still,
Quick to comfort
Truth-loving hearts in their mother tongue (to report
On the miracles She has wrought
In the U.K., the O.E.D.
Takes fourteen tomes): She suffers no evil,
And a statesman still, so her grace prevent, may keep a treaty,
A poor commoner arrive at
The Proper Name for his cat.

No hero is immortal till he dies:
Nor is a tongue.
But a lay of Beowulf's language too can be sung,
Ignoble, maybe, to the young,
Having no monsters and no gore
To speak of, yet not without its beauties
For those who have learned to hope: a lot of us are grateful for
What J. R. R. Tolkein has done
As bard to Anglo-Saxon.

III

ELEGY FOR J.F.K.
(November 22nd, 1963)

Why *then*, why *there*,
Why *thus*, we cry, did he die?
The heavens are silent.

What he was, he was:
What he is fated to become
Depends on us.

Remembering his death,
How we choose to live
Will decide its meaning.

When a just man dies,
Lamentation and praise,
Sorrow and joy, are one.

IV

LINES FOR ELIZABETH MAYER
*on the occasion
of her eightieth birthday,
April 6th, 1964*

Withdrawn from the Object-World
A Grand Duke's glass coach,
His Chaplain's *Sand-Uhr*,

And extinct
The governesses who played
Chopin, *Opus 31:*

(Two of the Six
Noble Gases have, I hear,
Already been seduced.)

While for those who still remember them,
The minutes are long,
The day short.

Here, now, as bodies,
We have no option:
Dates, locations divide us.

As You, as I, though, each
Is born with the right
Of liberal passage

To Dame Philology's Realm
Where, in singular,
Name may call to Name,

And Name to Name respond,
Untaunted by
Numerical haphazard.

So, today, I think that sound
To which you have answered
For eighty years

With this intent:
That you shall think it happily,
As *Elizabeth*

Through twenty-five has been
For a happiness of mine
Its Proper Name.

Deep in earth's opaque mirror,
The old oak's roots
Reflected its branches:

Astrologers in reverse,
Keen-eyed miners
Conned their scintillant gems.

❖ ❖ ❖

The underground roads
Are, as the dead prefer them,
Always tortuous.

❖ ❖ ❖

When he looked the cave in the eye,
Hercules
Had a moment of doubt.

❖ ❖ ❖

Fords may have demons,
But no spring is watched by
A malevolent nymph.

❖ ❖ ❖

The brook's impromptu babble
Suggested to Orpheus
A cunning song.

❖ ❖ ❖

The water of the sleeping lake
Dreamed kindly
Of earth and fire and air.

❖ ❖ ❖

The flowers danced for the wind
Gladly, knowing
That was all he needed.

❖ ❖ ❖

Metal, extorted from stone
In a paroxysm of fire,
Was beaten,

Then ducked in water:
Outrage sealed into the sword
Fury for battle.

❖ ❖ ❖

Old Brandy in the heated spoon
Looked dignified at first, but soon
Went off his head and, lost to shame,
Lay wallowing in a fit of flame.

❖ ❖ ❖

After Krakatoa exploded, the first living thing to return
Was the ant, Tridomyrex, seeking in vain its symbiot fern.

❖ ❖ ❖

To grow:—like the vine
That instinctively rations
Its water intake.

❖ ❖ ❖

Leaning out over
The dreadful precipice,
One contemptuous tree.

❖ ❖ ❖

Shod and saddled,
The horses of the Tartars
Could out-gallop the drought.

[61]

❖ ❖ ❖

Like spoiled rich women,
The swallows follow
Their congenial isotherm.

❖ ❖ ❖

When we fondle one,
Our other cats are jealous:
But they don't envy

Nor admire either,
Ignorant of why
Another can be more loved.

❖ ❖ ❖

Could any tiger
Drink martinis, smoke cigars,
And last as we do?

❖ ❖ ❖

Chirm and skimmer of insects
In the coy noon heat:
He smiled at himself.

❖ ❖ ❖

Self and Shadow:
By day a comic pair,
At moonprime one and somber.

❖ ❖ ❖

Flattered by Pleasure, accused by Pain,
Which of the two
Should he believe?

❖ ❖ ❖

To himself the Brute Fact:
To others (sometimes)
A useful metaphor.

Because the level table
Made him think of steppes,
He knew it was there.

❖ ❖ ❖

Like the redstart,
He recalls but a formless fragment
Of his real tune.

❖ ❖ ❖

A signpost points him out his road:
But names no place,
Numbers no distance.

❖ ❖ ❖

Not daring to saunter,
He made forced marches,
Uphill, against the wind.

❖ ❖ ❖

Hunting for some lost object
He was meant to forget,
He lost himself.

❖ ❖ ❖

Making it easy to boil,
The tinker's art
Ruined the tribe's cuisine.

❖ ❖ ❖

The yoke permitted
Gentle dray horses to build
Coercive castles.

❖ ❖ ❖

At chess, before gunpowder,
The Queen took only
Diagonal steps.

❖ ❖ ❖

From the Eastern Campaign
They returned with forks
And a more flamboyant rite.

❖   ❖   ❖

The iconoclast's home
Was hung with many
Pornographic pictures.

❖   ❖   ❖

Mental parasites,
They took up
A universal vague religion.

❖   ❖   ❖

How image today
The Knight's lonely Quest? On all roads
Laute Leute.

❖   ❖   ❖

Honest democrats,
They would die rather
Than touch their caps to a lord:

But they know better
Than to get fresh
With Customs & Immigration.

❖   ❖   ❖

Their lives were boring and undignified:
They worked a little, they consumed, they died.

❖   ❖   ❖

Life wrong already:
Each life an amateur sleuth,
Asking *Who did it?*

❖   ❖   ❖

Behind the perversions
Not lust for pleasure,
But a cry for justice.

❖ ❖ ❖

Finding Echo repellent,
Narcissus ate his snot,
Pee'd in his bath.

❖ ❖ ❖

Their daydreams were the same:
A blood brother, a comrade-in-arms,
Plus sex.

So were their natures:
Both wish to play *Officer*,
Neither *Other Ranks*.

❖ ❖ ❖

Loneliness waited
For Reality
To come through the glory hole.

❖ ❖ ❖

Cigars. Scotch.
They recalled (inexactly)
How many, how big, how much.

❖ ❖ ❖

Pride has always despised Pleasure,
Left gluttony, lust,
To underdogs:

Sought Joy and found it,
Taking life, destroying things,
Moving at high speed.

❖ ❖ ❖

The God of Love
Will never withdraw our right
To grief and infamy.

[65]

I

THE ROMANTIC

"Silly girl, listen!"
But she doesn't listen,
While the village roofs glisten
Bright in the sun.
"Silly girl, what do you do there,
As if there were someone to view there,
A face to gaze on and greet there,
A live form warmly to meet there,
When there is no one, none, do you hear!"
But she doesn't hear.

Like a dead stone
She stands there alone,
Staring ahead of her, peering around
For something that has to be found,
Till, suddenly spying it,
She touches it, clutches it,
Laughing and crying.

Is it you, my Johnny, my true love, my dear?
I knew you would never forget me,
Even in death! Come with me, let me
Show you the way, now! Hold your breath, though,
And tiptoe lest stepmother hear!

What can she hear? They have made him
A grave, two years ago laid him
Away with the dead.

Save me, Mother of God! I'm afraid.
But why? Why should I flee you now?
What do I dread?
Not Johnny! My Johnny won't hurt me.
It is my Johnny! I see you now,
Your eyes, your white shirt.

But it's pale as linen you are,
Cold as winter you are!
Let my lips take the cold from you,
Kiss the chill of the mould from you.

Dearest love, let me die with you,
In the deep earth lie with you,
For this world is dark and dreary,
I am lonely and weary!

Alone among the unkind ones,
Who mock at my vision,
My tears their derision,
Seeing nothing, the blind ones!

Dear God! A cock is crowing.
Whitely glimmers the dawn.
Johnny! Where are you going?
Don't leave me! I am forlorn.

So, caressing, talking aloud to her
Lover, she stumbles and falls,
And her cry of anguish calls
A pitying crowd to her.

"Cross yourselves! It is, surely,
Her Johnny come back from the grave:
While he lived, he loved her entirely.
May God his soul now save!"

Hearing what they are saying,
I, too, start praying.

"The girl is out of her senses!"
Shouts a man with a learned air,
"My eye and my lenses
Know there's nothing there.

"Ghosts are a myth
Of alewife and blacksmith.
Clodhoppers! This is treason
Against King Reason!"

"Yet the girl loves," I reply diffidently,
"And the people believe reverently:
Faith and love are more discerning
Than lenses or learning.

"You know the dead truths, not the living,
The world of things, not the world of loving.
Where does any miracle start?
Cold eye, look in your heart!"

                              (Adam Mickiewicz)

II

VOLCANOES

Extinct volcanoes are silent:
Ash chokes crater and vent.
There giants hide from the sun
After the evil they have done.

Realms ever denser and colder
Weigh on each brutal shoulder,
But the old wicked visions keep
Visiting them in their sleep.

They behold a city, sure
Her summer will endure,
Though columns carved from congealed
Lava frame garden and field.

It is long ago: in sunlit hours
Girls gather armfuls of flowers;
Bacchantes give a meaning sign
To men as they sip their wine.

A feast is in progress: louder
The diners grow, more heated and lewder . . .
O my Pompeii in your cindery grave,
Child of a princess and a slave!

What future did you assume,
What were you thinking of and whom,
When you leaned your elbow thus
Thoughtlessly on Vesuvius?

Were you carried away by his stories?
Did you gaze with astonished eyes?
Didn't you guess—were you *that* innocent?—
Passion can be violent?

And then, when that day ended,
Did he lay a knowing forehead
At your dead feet? Did he, didn't he,
Bellow: "Forgive me!"?

                                    (*Bella Akhmadulina*)

[69]

THE COMPLAINT BOOK

Every railroad station keeps a book for complaints,
And, if you ask for it, they have to give it you.
It wouldn't be a bad idea, I think,
If eternity had a book like that:
Then people wouldn't have to keep silent about their sorrow.
Timidly, cautiously at first, they would all come, bringing
The griefs they endure, the wrongs they are made to suffer,
To universal attention and judgment.
How we should then be struck, I know,
By one entry of half a line,
                                        written
By that woman who, slumped against its railings,
Was crying in the park last night.

                                        (*Evgeni Vinokurov*)

IV

PARABOLIC BALLAD

Along a parabola life like a rocket flies,
Mainly in darkness, now and then on a rainbow.
Redheaded bohemian Gauguin, the painter,
Started out life as a prosperous stockbroker:
In order to get to the Louvre from Montmartre,
He made a detour all through Java, Sumatra,
Tahiti, the Isles of Marquesas . . .
                                        With levity
He took off in flight from the madness of money,
The cackle of women, the frowst of academies,
Overpowered the force of terrestrial gravity.

The high priests drank their porter and kept up their jabbering:
"Straight lines are shorter, less steep than parabolas.
It's more proper to copy the heavenly mansions."

He rose like a howling rocket, insulting them
With a gale that tore off the tails of their frock coats,
So he didn't steal into the Louvre by the front door,
But on a parabola smashed through the ceiling.
In finding their truth lives vary in daring:
Worms come through holes, bold men on parabolas.

There once was a girl who lived in my neighborhood:
We went to one school, took exams simultaneously.
But I took off with a bang,
      I went whizzing
Through the prosperous double-faced stars of Tiflis.
Forgive me for this idiotic parabola.
Cold shoulders in a pitch-dark vestibule . . .
Rigid, erect, as a radio antenna rod,
Sending its call sign out through the freezing
Dark of the universe, how you rang out to me,
An undoubtable signal, an earthly standby,
From whom I might get my flight bearings to land by.
The parabola doesn't come to us easily.

Laughing at law with its warnings and paragraphs,
Art, love and history race along recklessly
Over a parabolic trajectory.

He is leaving tonight for Siberia.
      Perhaps
A straight line after all is the shorter one actually.
        (Andrei Voznesensky)

Unmarried, nearsighted, rather deaf,
This anonymous dwarf,
Legendary ancestor
Of Gunsmiths to His Majesty
And other bespoke houses:—
Every museum visitor knows him.

Excluded by his cave
From weather and events, he measures
Days by the job done, and at night
Dreams of the Perfect Object, war to him
A scarcity of bronze, the fall of princes
A change of customer.

Not a musician: songs
Encourage laboring demes, amuse the idle,
But would distract a self-appointed worker
From listening to his hammer's dactyl.
And not an orator: sophists
Don't do metallurgy.

His prices are high and, if he doesn't like you,
He won't oblige: once more the Quality
Are made to learn that charm is useless,
A threat fatal. He will deliver
In his good time, not yours: he has no rival,
And he knows you know it.

His love, embodied in each useful wonder,
Can't save them in our world from insult,
But may avenge it: beware, then, maladroit,
Thumb-sucking children of all ages,
Lest on your mangled bodies the court verdict
Be Death by Misadventure.

AT THE PARTY

Unrhymed, unrhythmical, the chatter goes:
Yet no one hears his own remarks as prose.

Beneath each topic tunelessly discussed
The ground-bass is reciprocal mistrust.

The names in fashion shuttling to and fro
Yield, when deciphered, messages of woe.

You cannot read me like an open book.

I'm more myself than you will ever look.

Will no one listen to my little song?

Perhaps I shan't be with you very long.

A howl for recognition, shrill with fear,
Shakes the jam-packed apartment, but each ear
Is listening to its hearing, so none hear.

LOST

Lost on a fogbound spit of sand
In shoes that pinched me, close at hand
I heard the plash of Charon's oar,
Who ferries no one to a happy shore.

A sweet tooth taught us to admire
The bees before we'd made a fire:
Nemorivagrant tribes at least
Could serve wild honey at a feast.

Accustomed in hard times to clem,
We started soon to envy them
An industry that stocks their shelves
With more food than they need themselves.

By Estimation, too, inclined
Towards a social stead of kind,
We sought from study of their hives
To draw some moral for our lives,

And when conspiracy, revolt,
Gave Princes of this world a jolt,
Philosopher and Christian Preacher
Upheld the Bee as Civics Teacher.

Now bestiaries are out, for now
Research has demonstrated how
They actually behave, they strike us
As being horridly unlike us:

Though some believe (some even plan
To do it) that from Urban Man,
By Advertising plus the aid
Of drugs, an insect might be made.

No. Who can learn to love his neighbor
From neuters whose one love is labor,
To rid his Government of knaves
From commonwealths controlled by slaves?

How, for us children of the word,
Anthropomorphic and absurd
To ask what code they satisfy
When they swoop out to sting and die,

Or what catharsis undergo
When they put on their biggest show,
A duel to the death between
A tooting and a quacking Queen.

If all a top physicist knows
About the Truth be true,
Then, for all the so-and-so's,
Futility and grime,
Our common world contains,
We have a better time
Than the Greater Nebulae do,
Or the atoms in our brains.

Marriage is rarely bliss
But, surely it would be worse
As particles to pelt
At thousands of miles per sec
About a universe
In which a lover's kiss
Would either not be felt
Or break the loved one's neck.

Though the face at which I stare
While shaving it be cruel
For, year after year, it repels
An aging suitor, it has,
Thank God, sufficient mass
To be altogether there,
Not an indeterminate gruel
Which is partly somewhere else.

Our eyes prefer to suppose
That a habitable place
Has a geocentric view,
That architects enclose
A quiet Euclidean space:
Exploded myths—but who
Would feel at home astraddle
An ever expanding saddle?

This passion of our kind
For the process of finding out
Is a fact one can hardly doubt,
But I would rejoice in it more
If I knew more clearly what
We wanted the knowledge for,
Felt certain still that the mind
Is free to know or not.

It has chosen once, it seems,
And whether our concern
For magnitude's extremes
Really become a creature
Who comes in a median size,
Or politicizing Nature
Be altogether wise,
Is something we shall learn.

ASCENSION DAY, 1964

From leaf to leaf in silence
The year's new green
Is passed along northward:

A bit, though, behind schedule,
For the chestnut chandeliers
Are still dim.

But today's atmosphere
Is encouraging,
And the orchard peoples,

Naïve in white
Or truculent in pink,
Aspect an indulgent blue.

Pleased with his one good remark,
A cuckoo repeats it,
Well-satisfied,

Some occasional heavy feeder
Obliges
With a florid song.

Lives content
With their ecological niche
And relevant objects,

Unable to tell
A hush before storms
From one after massacres,

As warriors, as lovers,
Without mixed feelings:
What is our feast to them?

This Thursday when we must
Go through the ritual
Formulae of farewell,

The words, the looks,
The embraces, knowing
That this time they are final.

Will as we may to believe
That parting should be
And that a promise

Of future joy can be kept,
Absence remains
The factual loss it is:

Here on out as permanent,
Obvious to all,
As the presence in each

Of a glum Kundry,
Impelled to giggle
At any crucifixion.

WHITSUNDAY IN KIRCHSTETTEN
(for H. A. Reinhold)

Grace dances. I would pipe. Dance ye all.
—Acts of John

Komm Schöpfer Geist I bellow as Herr Beer
picks up our slim offerings and Pfarrer Lustkandl
    quietly gets on with the Sacrifice
as Rome does it: outside car-worshipers enact
    the ritual exodus from Vienna
their successful cult demands (though reckoning time
    by the Jewish week and the Christian year
like their pedestian fathers). When Mass is over,
    although obedient to Canterbury,
I shall be well gruss-gotted, asked to contribute
    to *Caritas*, though a metic come home
to lunch on my own land: no doubt, if the Allies had not
    conquered the Ost-Mark, if the dollar fell,
the *Gemütlichkeit* would be less, but when was peace
    or its concomitant smile the worse
for being undeserved?

                    In the onion-tower overhead
    bells clash at the Elevation, calling
on Austria to change: whether the world has improved
    is doubtful, but we believe it could
and the divine Tiberius didn't. Rejoice, the bells
    cry to me. Blake's Old Nobodaddy
in his astronomic telescopic heaven,
    the Big White Christian upstairs, is dead,
and won't come hazing us no more, nor bless our bombs:
    no more need sons of the menalty,
divining their future from plum stones, count aloud
    Army, Navy, Law, Church, nor a Prince
say who is *papabile*. (The Ape of the Living God

[82]

knows how to stage a funeral, though,
as penitents like it: Babel, like Sodom, still
   has plenty to offer, though of course it draws
a better sort of crowd.) Rejoice: we who were born
   congenitally deaf are able
to listen now to rank outsiders. The Holy Ghost
   does not abhor a golfer's jargon,
a Lower-Austrian accent, the cadences even
   of my own little Anglo-American
musico-literary set (though difficult,
   saints at least may think in algebra
without sin): but no sacred nonsense can stand Him.
   Our magic syllables melt away,
our tribal formulae are laid bare: since this morning,
   it is with a vocabulary
made wholesomely profane, open in lexicons
   to our foes to translate, that we endeavor
each in his idiom to express the true *magnalia*
   which need no hallowing from us, loaning terms,
exchanging graves and legends. (Maybe, when just now
   Kirchstetten prayed for the dead, only I
remembered Franz Joseph the Unfortunate, who danced
   once in eighty-six years and never
used the telephone.)

                  An altar bell makes a noise
   as the Body of the Second Adam
is shown to some of his torturers, forcing them
   to visualize absent enemies
with the same right to grow hybrid corn and be wicked
   as an Abendlander. As crows fly,
ninety kilometers from here our habits end,
   where minefield and watchtower say NO EXIT
from peace-loving Crimtartary, except for crows
   and agents of peace: from Loipersbach

to the Bering Sea not a living stockbroker,
   and church attendance is frowned upon
like visiting brothels (but the chess and physics
   are still the same). We shall bury you
and dance at the wake, say her chiefs: that, says Reason
   is unlikely. But to most people
I'm the wrong color: it could be the looter's turn
   for latrine duty and the flogging block,
my kin who trousered Africa, carried our smell
   to germless poles.
                Down a Gothic nave
comes our Pfarrer now, blessing the West with water:
   we may go. There is no Queen's English
in any context for *Geist* or *Esprit*: about
   catastrophe or how to behave in one
I know nothing, except what everyone knows—
   if there when Grace dances, I should dance.

ABOUT THE AUTHOR

WYSTAN HUGH AUDEN *was born in York, England, in 1907. He has been a resident of the United States since 1939, and an American citizen since 1946. Educated at Gresham's School, Holt, and at Christ Church, Oxford, he became associated with a small group of young writers in London—among them Stephen Spender and Christopher Isherwood —who became recognized as the most promising of the new generation in English letters. He collaborated with Isherwood on the plays* The Dog Beneath the Skin, The Ascent of F-6 *and* On the Frontier, *as well as on* Journey to a War, *a prose record of experience in China. He has edited many anthologies, including* The Oxford Book of Light Verse *and, with Norman Holmes Pearson,* Poets of the English Language. *In collaboration with Chester Kallman, he has also written the libretto for Igor Stravinsky's opera,* The Rake's Progress, *and for Hans Henze's opera,* Elegy for Young Lovers. *His selected essays,* The Dyer's Hand, *appeared in 1962.*

Mr. Auden is the author of several volumes of poetry, including The Double Man, For the Time Being, The Age of Anxiety, Nones, *and* The Shield of Achilles, *which received the National Book Award in 1956. That same year he was elected Professor of Poetry at Oxford University. His* Selected Poetry *appears in* The Modern Library. Homage to Clio *was published in 1960.*